Echo Show 5 User Manual and Setup Guide

Simplified Steps for Setting Up and Maximizing Your Show 5 with Illustrations

By

Patrick Izzo

Table of Content

Table of Content 2

Introduction..5

Chapter 1 .... **6**

Setting Up Your Show 5...6

Connect Mobile Devices to Echo Show 5 9

Setting up Amazon Household..11

Powering the Echo Show..15

Chapter 2 ....**17**

Configure Echo Show 5 17

Connect to the Alexa App 21

Navigate your Echo Show 5...21

Modify settings 22

Reset Echo Show 5..23

Hard reset 24

Set up Alexa profiles. 25

    Methods for Creating Alexa Profiles...............................26

Modifying Alexa's settings..31

Household Profiles 32

Chapter 3 ....**36**

Play Music..36

Listen to Music with Bluetooth 39

Remove Profanity Music 40

Listen to Podcasts 43

Play Audiobooks.. 46

Listen to Radio 47

Equalize your Echo Show Sound 48

Chapter 4..**50**

Configure calling and messaging 50

Add Contacts 53

Import single Contacts 56

Video call 61

Set Up a Group Call... 63

Initiate Group Video Calling.. 64

Enhanced video calling Features.................................. 64

Tips for video calls 65

Fast calling 66

Home Monitoring 66

Home monitoring Privacy concerns............................. 68

Chapter 5..**70**

What are Alexa Routines.. 70

Customize Alexa Routine 71

Fantastic Alexa Routines 72

Welcome Home... 75

Traffic Report 76

Share routines 77

Create Voice ID 78

Teach Alexa your voice. 81

Verify Name Pronunciation 81

Chapter 6 .... **83**

Connect Music Streaming Platforms 83

Add Spotify 83

Add Pandora 85

Include Deezer 86

Create IFTTT Account 87

Modify Background 91

Configure Silks settings 92

Adjust sounds Levels 93

Karaoke 94

Set screen brightness 95

Watch YouTube 96

Update software 98

Configure Netflix App 99

Connect Wi-Fi to Alexa 102

Modify Wi-Fi settings 103

Conclusion **104**

Introduction

The Amazon Echo Show 5 is a compact 5.5-inch touchscreen device with dimensions of 8.6 x 14.8 x 7.3 cm and a weight of 410g. It features a 1-megapixel front camera for 720p HD video calls, a built-in microphone, and a USB port for charging. The device has a textured finish and a rubber base. On the top, you'll find buttons for volume control, a microphone area, and a camera privacy switch, providing peace of mind that you can block the camera when needed.

Behind the device, there's a 2-watt speaker, a power port, a USB input, and a 3.5mm headphone jack. While the sound quality may not match high-end Bluetooth speakers, it's generally acceptable for most users. For a richer bass experience, you can connect the Echo Show 5 to an external Bluetooth device. While it may not be ideal for watching full HD movies, it handles video clips well.

The standout feature of the Echo Show 5 is the Alexa app, which allows you to control nearly all of the device's functions with voice commands. Whether you're in the kitchen and need to pause music with wet hands or want to monitor your baby's room or see who's at the door, Alexa can assist you. This guide provides detailed information to help you set up and make the most of your Amazon Echo Show 5.

CHAPTER 1

Setting Up Your Show 5

Setting up your Echo Show 5 is pretty straightforward, especially if you have a reliable internet connection. To complete the setup, you'll need an Amazon account, which you can easily create on the Amazon website if you don't already have one.

Here's a step-by-step guide to setting up your Echo Show 5:

1. Plug the power cable into the power port to initiate the setup process.
2. Once the device powers on, it will display available Wi-Fi networks to connect to.
3. Connect your Echo Show 5 to your Wi-Fi network. You may need to enter the network password. Alternatively,

you can use your phone's Wi-Fi hotspot for connectivity. Remember that a stable internet connection is essential for the device to function effectively.

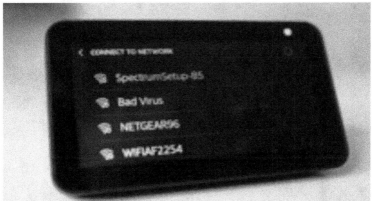

4. After successfully connecting to your network, you'll see a "CONTINUE" button below the screen.
5. Tap the "CONTINUE" button, and the setup wizard will prompt you to enter your Amazon account email and password. If you don't have an Amazon account, there's a link on the screen to create one.

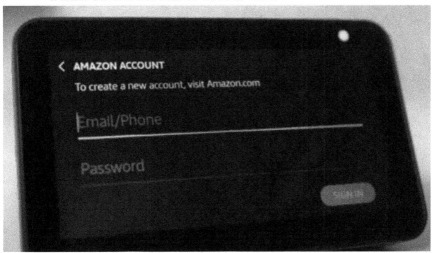

6. Once you've logged into your Amazon account, a message will confirm your successful login.

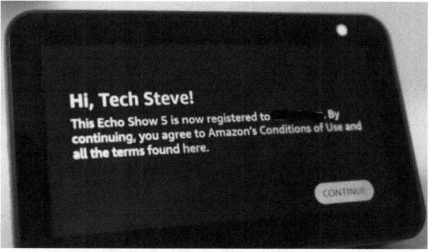

7. Tap "CONTINUE" to proceed.
8. You'll have the option to change the time zone and location. Make your selections and then select "CONTINUE."

9. Optionally, you can add your Echo Show 5 to a group, such as the room where you intend to place the device. This step is skippable if you prefer.

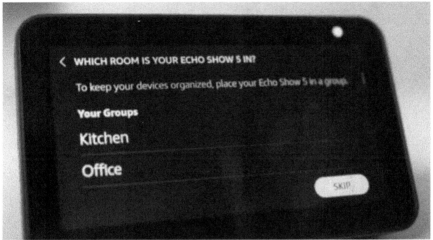

10. If you add it to a group, you must name the device. Feel free to choose any name you like, but if you have multiple Echo devices, make sure their names are distinct.
11. The device may prompt you to update; in that case, select "DOWNLOAD AND INSTALL." A constant internet connection is crucial, allowing the Echo Show 5 to download and install updates automatically.
12. After completing the update, a screen will display the word "ECHO," and a voice prompt will confirm that "THIS DEVICE IS READY."

Connect Mobile Devices to Echo Show 5

The Echo Show 5 offers versatile connectivity with mobile devices, allowing you to enjoy various functions. Here are some of the functions that the Show 5 can perform when connected to a mobile device:

1. You can connect your Echo Show 5 to your mobile device via Bluetooth and use it to play music from your phone. To do this, follow these steps:
   - Swipe on the Echo Show 5 screen to reveal the notification panel.
   - Tap the settings icon on the left, next to the "Do Not Disturb" icon.
   - Select "Bluetooth," which is the first setting you'll see.
   - Enable Bluetooth on your phone and pair it with the Echo Show 5.
   - Start playing music directly from your phone.
2. You can use your mobile device as a portable Wi-Fi hotspot for your Echo Show 5. It lets you access the internet using your phone's cellular service carrier. To connect your Echo Show to your phone's portable Wi-Fi hotspot, follow these steps:
   - Go to "Settings" on your phone and turn on the portable Wi-Fi hotspot. If this is your first time using it, you may need to set it up.
   - Enter your preferred hotspot name and password, then tap "SAVE."
   - Turn on the Wi-Fi hotspot.
   - On your Echo Show, swipe down to reveal the Notification Panel.
   - Select the settings icon at the top right corner.
   - Find the "NETWORK" option just below the Bluetooth option.
   - Tap on it to view the list of available networks.

- Your phone's hotspot name will appear; tap on it.
- Enter the password if required.
3. You can connect your mobile device to the Echo Show 5 through the Alexa app, available for download from the Google Play Store or the Apple App Store (for iOS devices). The Alexa app provides access to many of the same features as the Echo Show 5 and allows you to control various aspects of your smart home. Additionally, you can use the Alexa app to connect certain home electronics to the Echo Show 5.

These connectivity options enhance your Echo Show 5 functionality and provide you with more ways to interact with and control your smart devices.

Setting up Amazon Household

Amazon Household is a fantastic feature that enables you to connect with your family members, fostering interaction and sharing Amazon Prime benefits among them. You can link at least two adults, four teens, and four children to a household account, creating a shared digital space for your family. While you cannot directly add children from the Alexa app, there's a separate process.

Sharing Amazon Prime benefits with your household members opens up various advantages, such as Amazon Photos and the ability to share photo albums, access to select books through Prime Reading, and more. So, how do you add members to your Amazon Household to start sharing content? Follow these straightforward steps. (Note: Any member wishing to join an

Amazon Household must have an Amazon account; if not, they can create one.)

1. Begin by logging into the Alexa app through your Echo device or phone (using your phone is recommended).

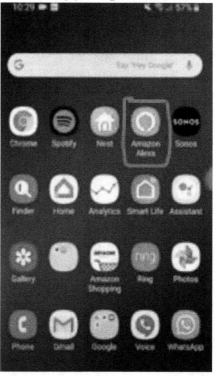

2. Once logged into the Alexa app, find the "Settings" option at the bottom of the screen and tap on it.

3. Select "Alexa's Account," then choose "Amazon Household."

4. You will need the Amazon account details of the adults who wish to join the household.

5. To add an adult or a teenager, they must provide their registered Amazon email and password.

6. If the adult already has an Amazon account, enter their details to verify their account. If not, they can create one by tapping the "Tap here to create an Amazon account" link.

7. The next screen will display a welcoming message for the new member. Tap the "JOIN HOUSEHOLD" button to proceed.
8. The new member must complete the process by logging into the Alexa app from any other device. If both of you want to use the same device, log out, and the new member can log in with their details.
9. The screen will display the names that have been added. New members can tap on their name, and from that point on, they can enjoy Alexa's skills and respond to requests.

If you intend to add a child to your Amazon Household, the process differs slightly from adding an adult. You must activate "Freetime" and set it up by adding the child to your device. To add a child to your Alexa device, follow these steps:

1. Once logged into your Alexa app, tap on "DEVICES" at the bottom of the screen.
2. Select "ECHO AND ALEXA" to view a list of connected devices.
3. Choose the specific Echo device you want to connect with the child.

After completing these steps, the next action is to enable FREETIME. Activating and managing FREETIME. To do that, follow the steps below:

1. On the menu screen, locate and select the FREETIME icon located below the screen.
2. Enable FREETIME by using the available switch.
3. A screen will appear explaining the features of FREETIME. Select "SETUP AMAZON FREE-TIME" to proceed.

4. You'll be presented with various options to customize the experience. You can turn off specific features such as calling and Drop-in, explicit music filters, and more.
5. Once you've configured the settings to your preference, select "CONTINUE." A short video showcasing Echo Dots Kids Edition may play.
6. If the video plays, you can cancel it by tapping the X icon at the top right corner of the screen.

Once you've completed the setup for the child, the Echo Show 5 will automatically switch to their account. You can then manage the child's profile settings using the AMAZON PARENT DASHBOARD, where you can monitor all their activities with the Echo device.

To switch between adult accounts, tell Alexa to do it by saying, "Alexa, switch account to (Name of account)." Alexa will switch to the specified adult account. Please note that you cannot switch directly between child and adult accounts. If you want to switch to a child account, you must follow the above mentioned process to activate it.

If you ever wish to turn off the FREETIME option, you can follow the same process you used to enable it.

Powering the Echo Show

The Echo Show 5 is designed to be powered through a dedicated power port, as it doesn't have an internal battery.

To turn on the device, plug the power cable into an electrical outlet and connect the cable to the power port at the back of the

Show 5. It ensures that the Show 5 remains connected to a power source properly.

CHAPTER 2

Configure Echo Show 5

Setting up your Echo Show is a straightforward process allowing you to enjoy the full range of features and functionalities this smart device offers.

1. Connect your Echo Show to an electrical outlet using the provided power adapter. The Echo Show does not have an internal battery, so it needs a constant power source to operate.
2. Once the device is powered on, the Echo Show's touchscreen will prompt you to choose your preferred language. You can easily make your selection by tapping on the screen. You can swipe down to reveal more language options if your language isn't listed.
3. Next, you'll need to connect your Echo Show to your Wi-Fi network. Choose your network from the list and enter the Wi-Fi password. A handy feature lets you view the password as you type it by tapping "Show" next to the text box. You can also decide whether to save the Wi-Fi password to your Amazon account for future convenience.

4. You must sign in with your Amazon account to access the full suite of Amazon services and features. If you don't have one, you can create it on another device with web access.

5. Confirm your Amazon account and accept Amazon's terms and conditions for device usage.

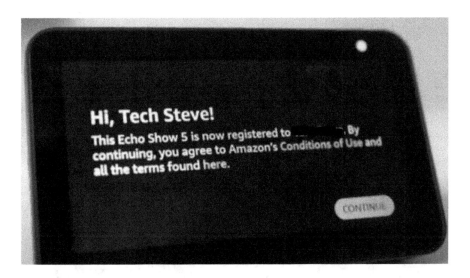

6. You can select the location of your Echo Show during the setup process. It helps categorize and manage all of your Amazon-connected smart home devices. If you prefer, you can skip this step and adjust the setting later.

7. Give your Echo Show a unique name, or use the pre-set name provided. Using a simple and distinct name can make it easier to use voice commands.

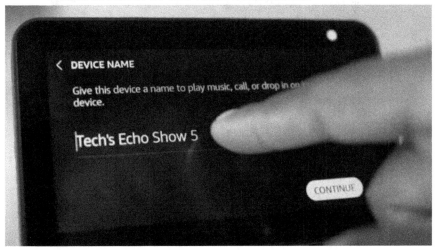

8. The setup process allows you to make various additional preferences, such as enabling the Echo Show's camera for surveillance. You can also choose whether to enable Amazon Sidewalk, which allows your device to broadcast its Wi-Fi network to other Alexa devices, ensuring they maintain a constant connection.

9. If children use your Echo Show primarily, you can select "Yes" to enable kid-friendly features like bedtime restrictions, usage logs, and content filters.

10. The setup process may prompt you regarding advertisements. You can opt out of these advertisements for a more ad-free experience.

Once you've completed these steps, your Echo Show will be fully set up and ready for use. Depending on the speed of your Wi-Fi connection, the screen may stay on "Almost Done" for a short period as the device completes the setup process.

Connect to the Alexa App

When you've associated your Echo Show with the same Amazon account, you'll find that it seamlessly integrates with the Alexa app. After the setup, your Echo Show will be readily visible within the Alexa app interface. You can locate it within your previously established group by navigating to "Devices" and selecting "Echo & Alexa."

In the Alexa app, managing the settings for your Echo Show is straightforward. To access and customize these settings, tap on the gear icon in the app's upper right corner.

Furthermore, the Echo Show extends its functionality beyond just voice commands. It empowers you to have control over various aspects, such as adjusting the volume to your preference. You can also utilize the built-in camera to view a live feed, allowing you to monitor your surroundings conveniently. Additionally, setting alarms on the Echo Show is a breeze, adding to its versatility and utility in your daily life.

Navigate your Echo Show 5

To access the primary menu on your Echo Show, initiate a leftward swipe from the upper right corner of the screen. Once done, a menu will appear, offering a multitude of actions to choose from, including playing music, watching videos, making video calls, and managing your smart home devices.

On your Echo Show, engaging in a video call can be seamlessly accomplished by executing a leftward swipe from the top right edge and selecting the "Communicate" option. You can tap "Dialer," located in the upper right corner, or opt for "Call" to initiate a call with a specific contact. Alternatively, you can effortlessly begin playing music by uttering the command, "Alexa, play [song]," or you can achieve the same result by swiping left from the right side of the screen, thereby entering the Music app. This action will unveil on-screen controls, allowing you to play, rewind, and skip tracks easily.

If you're interested in enjoying a video on your Echo Show, simply activate it by saying, "Alexa, watch." For this, initiate a leftward swipe from the right side of the screen to access the Video option. The subsequent step involves subscribing to a streaming service and selecting captivating content.

Moreover, if you wish to explore YouTube content, a simple voice command like "Alexa, search YouTube for..." will yield relevant results that you can indulge in on your Echo Show. Additionally, it's worth noting that you can also utilize the integrated Silk web browser to access YouTube videos. However, this approach may pose challenges due to the touch screen's limited precision.

Modify settings

To access the settings menu on your Echo Show, follow these simple steps: Begin by swiping down from the top of the screen and tap the cogwheel icon. This action will unveil various customization options within the settings menu, allowing you to make various adjustments. For instance, you can switch between different Wi-Fi networks and personalize your device by altering the wallpaper, among other customization possibilities.

Reset Echo Show 5

To access the settings on your Echo Show, you have a couple of convenient options. Firstly, you can employ voice command and say, "Go to settings," for an effortless entry into the settings menu. Alternatively, a tactile approach involves swiping down from the top of the display, which will also lead you to the settings interface.

Once inside the settings menu, possibilities await you, enabling you to tailor your gadget to your precise preferences. Among the array of options at your disposal, you can choose to initiate a reset by selecting the "Restore Default Settings" option. This choice presents you with further alternatives, allowing you to opt for "Return to Default Settings, but Keep Connected Smart

Home Devices." This nuanced control level ensures you can fine-tune your device to suit your specific needs.

Configuring your gadget becomes seamless as you follow the prompts on the screen. These prompts serve as a guiding hand, ensuring that you can effortlessly navigate the settings landscape.

However, if restarting your device didn't resolve the issue you were facing, or if you have decided to part ways with it, it's advisable to follow this important tip and remove the device from your Amazon account. You effectively sever the device's connection to your account by doing so. The device's settings will be wiped entirely clean, ensuring a clean break from its previous configuration.

Hard reset

1. Begin by switching on your device, ensuring that it's powered on and ready for the reset procedure.
2. Next, press and hold the Mute and Volume Down buttons simultaneously. Maintain this press until you observe the Amazon logo appearing on the screen. This step may take approximately a minute and a half, so exercise patience.
3. Your gadget will automatically begin rebooting once the Amazon logo graces the screen. Allow it to complete this reboot sequence.
4. Congratulations! The factory reset of your device has been successfully executed. You can now resume using your device with Alexa voice commands as usual.

Set up Alexa profiles.

Amazon offers two distinct methods for enabling multiple individuals to make the most of a shared Echo device. The first approach involves the creation of Alexa Profiles, which personalizes the voice assistant's responses to each user's unique preferences and needs.

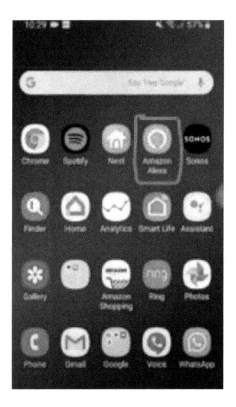

Imagine a scenario where you create a tailored Alexa profile for your wife. This profile equips her with the capability to perform tasks like placing a call to "Mom." Remarkably, the virtual assistant discerns that, in this context, "Mom" refers to your mother-in-law, not your own mother. Consequently, when your wife initiates a call to "Mom," the Echo device identifies the caller as your mother-in-law, and her name, rather than yours, appears on the caller ID. This seamless and intuitive differentiation ensures that interactions with the device are efficient and highly personalized.

Furthermore, the voice assistant considers individual preferences with Alexa Profiles when delivering news updates. It filters out previously reported news, providing quick summaries tailored to each user's specific interests and prior interactions.

Alternatively, the second option Amazon offers is the creation of Household Profiles. This approach allows multiple household members to link their Amazon accounts to your Echo or Echo Show device. This interconnected setup opens up a realm of shared resources and experiences within the household. Now, everyone can enjoy listening to each other's music libraries, delve into each other's audiobooks, and even collaborate on shared to-do lists, fostering communal engagement and convenience within the household environment.

Methods for Creating Alexa Profiles

To ensure that every member of your household enjoys personalized access to music, messages, and flash briefing on your Echo device, creating individual Alexa Profiles is a wise choice. It allows each member to tailor their experience to their specific preferences. Here's how to set up these profiles:

1. Commence the process by launching the Alexa app on your device.

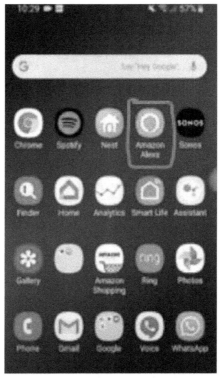

2. At the bottom of the app, you'll spot the "More" link in the footer. Click on it to unveil additional settings and options.

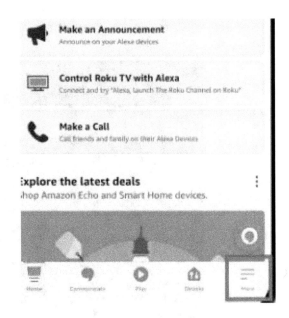

3. Within the expansive settings menu, delve into your device's specific settings.

4. In this device settings section, you'll discover "Your Profile and Family." It is the central hub where you can manage your Amazon account and the associated profiles.

5. Tap the "Add someone else" option to add another household member. It is where you'll find a list of users whose profiles are already linked to other Amazon products, such as Prime Video.

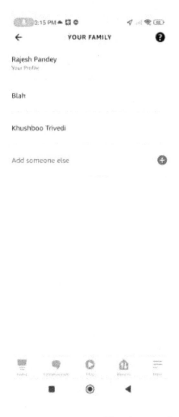

6. You can select an existing profile from the list or use the "Add" button to create a brand-new one. If you opt for the latter, enter the preferred name for the new profile, and then proceed by selecting "Next."

It enhances the personalization of their Echo device experience and ensures that everyone can fully enjoy the array of features offered by Alexa. Please bear in mind that sharing the smart speaker with others necessitates having their own Amazon accounts.

Modifying Alexa's settings

Your Amazon Echo and other Alexa-enabled devices are on the verge of gaining access to an enhanced Alexa Profile feature, promising an enriched user experience. With this update, you can tap into a user's profile, customizing it by adding a nickname and specifying your relationship with that user. This addition of personalization is set to elevate the calling and messaging services Alexa provides.

To make the most of this feature, the second user with an Alexa Profile must activate Voice ID through the Alexa mobile app on their device. Ensuring they log in to the app using the same Amazon ID originally used to set up the Echo device is essential. Here's a step-by-step guide to facilitate this process:

1. Begin by launching the Alexa app on your mobile device.

2. Connect your Echo gadget to your Amazon account and sign in.

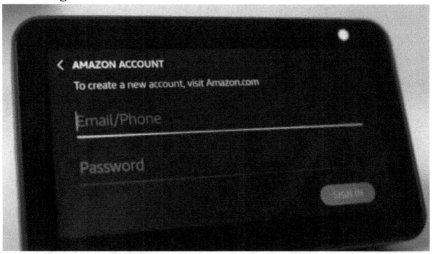

3. Once logged in, navigate to the available Alexa Profiles, which should be displayed in the app.
4. Select your name from the list. At this point, a prompt will appear, inviting you to create a Voice ID.
5. If you agree to proceed, choose the "Continue" option.
6. Grant the necessary permissions for the program to access the required settings.
7. You can manually initiate this process if you don't receive a prompt to activate Voice ID. Open the Alexa app, access the "More" menu, then navigate to "Settings," followed by "Your Profile & Family." Finally, select your name to enable Voice ID.

Household Profiles

Household Profiles offer the flexibility to include one more adult and accommodate up to four younger members within your household. Here's how to set up and manage these profiles:

1. Commence the process by launching the Alexa mobile app on your device.

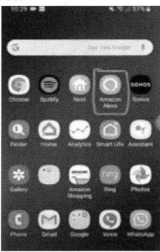

2. Look for the "More" link in the app's footer and click on it to reveal additional settings and options.

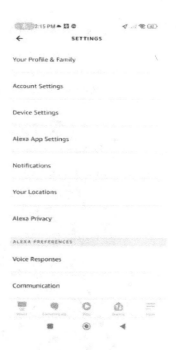

3. Under the Settings section, you'll find the "Household Profile" option. Select it to initiate the setup process.

4. Click the "Start" button to share your Echo device with a close relative. They will need to accept your invitation to join your household.

5. If you intend to include a different adult, teenager, or child in your Prime account and Echo, you can visit the Amazon Household website on a personal computer. The same procedures apply when welcoming teenagers into the family. However, children under 12 require a manual profile creation process.

Once you've successfully configured Household Profiles, you'll have the convenience of switching between profiles by simply saying, "Alexa, switch accounts." You can also inquire about the active account by asking, "Alexa, which account is this?" This way, you can seamlessly manage and utilize the Echo device within your household while ensuring each member enjoys their personalized experience.

CHAPTER 3

Play Music

Utilizing your Echo Show, you can seamlessly stream your favorite music playlist from various sources, including your smartphone, Bluetooth devices, and a wide array of popular streaming services like Apple Music, Amazon Music, Spotify, and many others.

Suppose you'd like to stream a specific track from these streaming services. To achieve this, follow these steps:

1. Open the Alexa app and click on the "More" button.

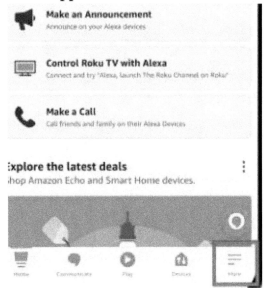

2. Next, select "Settings."

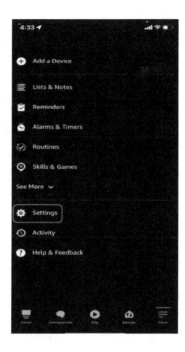

3. In the settings menu, choose "Music & Podcasts."

4. After that, click on "Link New Service."

5. Now, pick the music service you want to integrate.

Once you've successfully linked your Echo Show with your preferred streaming service and are ready to start playing a song, you can use the voice command "Alexa, play Lady Gaga." Alternatively, you can select your Echo Show as the output device within your music application and initiate streaming from there.

Here's a detailed guide on how to set up music streaming on your Echo Show through your preferred music application, such as Deezer:

1. If you wish to add a streaming service like Deezer to your Echo Show, select it from the "Link New Service" menu.
2. In the skills menu, choose the "Enable to Use" option. Then, provide your Deezer account information along with the necessary permissions.
3. After successfully configuring your Deezer account, return to the Spotify skill menu and select "Done."
4. Proceed to "Default Services," and choose your preferred streaming service as the default option.

Whenever you request Alexa to play a specific track, it will automatically do so from your chosen default streaming service, ensuring a seamless and customized music streaming experience on your Echo Show.

Listen to Music with Bluetooth

Unlocking the potential to stream your cherished music tracks directly from your Bluetooth-enabled devices to your Echo Show is a convenient and enjoyable experience. You have two methods at your disposal for pairing your devices. The first involves a voice command – ensure your Bluetooth device is in pairing mode and then instruct your Echo Show with the phrase, "Alexa, pair." It prompts your Echo Show to initiate the pairing process, after which you'll need to access the Bluetooth settings menu on your smartphone, where you can select your Echo Show from the list of available devices. Alexa will provide you with a confirmation when the connection is successfully established.

The manual pairing method is equally straightforward for those who prefer a more hands-on approach. Open the Alexa app, navigate to the "Devices" section, and select "Echo and Alexa." Choose the Echo device you wish to pair with your phone from there. On the subsequent interface, opt for "Pair Alexa Gadget." Then, venture into the Bluetooth settings menu on your smartphone, locate your Echo Show in the list of available devices, and complete the connection. Once your devices are paired, you can launch your music application on your phone and select a track, which will seamlessly begin playing on your Echo Show, elevating your music streaming experience.

Should you ever need to sever this connection between your Echo Show and your phone, all it takes is the simple voice command, "Alexa, disconnect from [your device name]." It ensures you maintain complete control over your music streaming with your Echo Show, whether you opt for voice-guided or manual pairing, enhancing your audio experience with ease and flexibility.

Remove Profanity Music

To ensure a family-friendly environment on your Echo Show and prevent your kids from encountering inappropriate content, follow these simple steps:

1. Open the Alexa app.

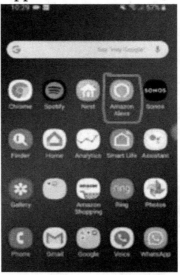

2. Tap the "More" button.

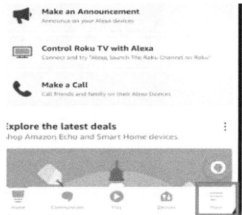

3. Select "Settings."

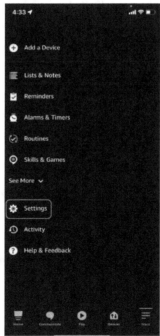

4. Under the "Preferences" section, click on "Music & Podcasts."

5. Now, tap the "Explicit Language Filter" option.

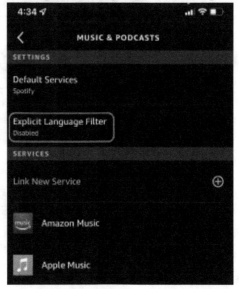

6. Toggle Explicit Filter on. It will help filter out obscene content.

Listen to Podcasts

If you'd like to stream music directly from the Alexa app on your mobile device, you can do so with these steps:

1. Launch the Alexa app.

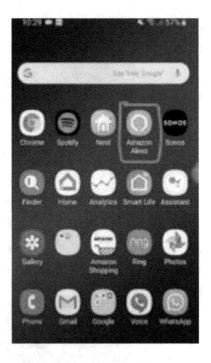

2. Tap the "More" button.

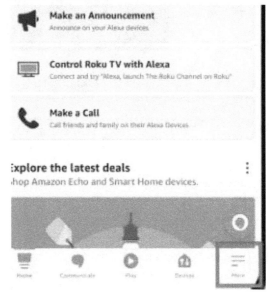

3. Select Settings.

4. Then, select "Music & Podcasts."

5. Choose your preferred music service, such as "Deezer," under "Music."

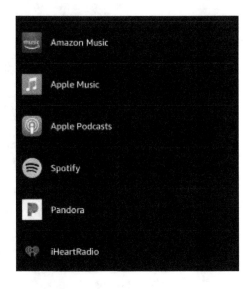

6. Then, select "Podcasts."

7. Use the search field or browse through categories to find your desired podcast show.

8. From the upper section of the app, choose your preferred speakers, and then tap the podcast show's cover to start playing it. This way, you can enjoy music and podcasts seamlessly using your Alexa app and Echo Show while maintaining a family-friendly and filtered content environment.

Play Audiobooks

Audiobooks offer an enjoyable and convenient way to immerse yourself in literature, and with your Alexa-enabled device, you can have Alexa read them aloud. Here's how to make the most of this feature:

1. Launch the Alexa app and tap the "Play" button at the lower edge of the display. Swipe to "Audible Library."

2. Select the audiobook you wish to listen to.
3. Choose the specific Echo device on which you want to hear the audiobook.
4. To have Alexa read the content aloud, either tap the play button on the audiobook or use the voice command, "Alexa, read [the book's title]."

Listen to Radio

1. Open the Alexa app.

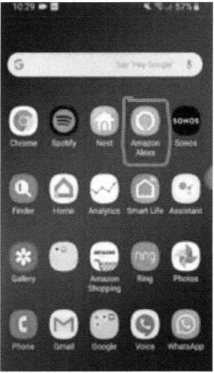

2. Tap on the "More" button.

47

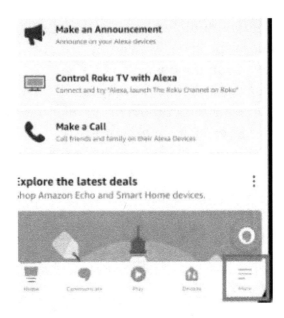

3. Select "Skills & Games" and either search for the desired skill or choose from various categories like "Music & Audio" or "News" to explore the available stations and skills.
4. Choose the skill you prefer and click "Enable Skill."
5. Then, select "Launch." Alternatively, you can use the voice command, "Alexa, open skills," and specify the skill you want to activate. Follow the on-screen prompts to make your selection.
6. You can listen to local stations without enabling skills by simply using the command, "Alexa, play [station's name]."

Equalize your Echo Show Sound

1. Swipe down from the upper area of your Echo Show.
2. Select the Settings button.

3. Tap on "Sounds."
4. From there, click on "Equalizer."
5. In the Equalizer menu, you can adjust the bass, treble, and more to fine-tune your audio experience.
6. If you prefer voice commands, say, "Alexa, increase/reduce the bass," or ask it to reset the equalizer settings. This way, you can effortlessly tailor your Echo Show's sound to your preferences.

CHAPTER 4

Configure calling and messaging

Before you can engage in video or audio calls using your Echo device, activating communications features is imperative. Here's how to enable these functionalities:

1. Start by selecting "Devices" at the bottom of your device's display.
2. Navigate to "Echo & Alexa" in the menu bar that appears.
3. Choose the specific Echo Show device you wish to utilize.
4. Access the device's settings by clicking the gear icon in the upper right corner.
5. Within the settings menu, look for "General" and select it to access the Communications settings.
6. To activate Communications, slide the switch to the "On" position. If you wish to enable "Drop-in," you can also select it from the drop-down menu.

To unlock Alexa's premium functions, follow these steps to download the app:

1. Select "More" from the bottom menu on your device's screen.

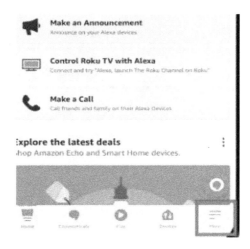

2. Within the "Preferences" menu, opt for the "Communications" option in the Alexa settings menu.

3. Select "Enhanced Features."

4. In the "Enhanced Features" section, turn on the setting by toggling the "Enabled" button.

For successful participation in video conversations, all individuals involved must have both "Communications" and "Enhanced Features" turned on within their respective Alexa apps. By following these steps, you'll be well-equipped to enjoy the full communication features available on your Echo device.

Add Contacts

1. Open the Alexa app on your device.

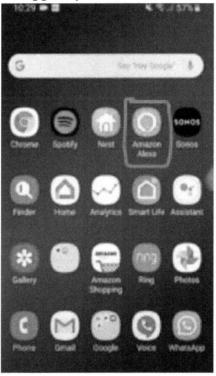

2. Confirm that the individuals you wish to include in your group are already in your contacts list within the Alexa app.
3. Go to the "Communication" settings in the Alexa app.

4. Locate the option labeled "Drop-In."

5. Verify that it is turned on for each person you want to be part of the group. It ensures that they can receive Drop-In calls.

If your primary goal is to create a calling group, you can proceed to the next section of the process. However, if you're interested in importing your phonebook contacts into the Alexa app's Communication settings, here's how you can do it:

1. Under "Import Contacts" in the Alexa app's Communication settings, select "Import Contacts."
2. Switch to the "On" position to initiate the contact import process.

3. Your entire phonebook will be synchronized with the Amazon service immediately, making it easier to connect with your contacts using Alexa's communication features.

Import single Contacts

You have a couple of options to add contacts individually for calling someone not already in your Amazon address book, whether using your Amazon Echo Show or the Alexa app on your smartphone. Here's how you can do it via the Alexa app:

1. Open the Alexa app on your smartphone.

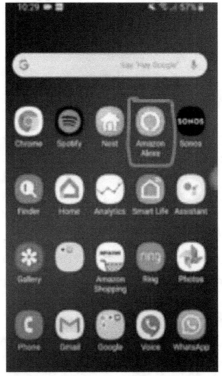

2. At the bottom of the app, select the "Communication," which should be located near the lower part of the screen.

3. Now, select the "People" button represented by the person icon on the far right.

4. Choose "Add Contact" from the menu when you click the three dots in the top right corner. Alternatively, you can opt for "Add New" under your name in the contact list.

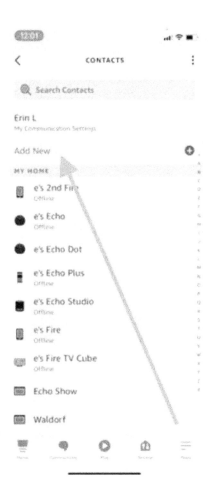

5. Select the option to add a contact.
6. Provide the name, nickname, and relationship (so you can say "Call my mom" or "Call my GF") of the person you intend to call.
7. Enter their cell phone number and click the "Save" button to confirm the addition.
8. Once you've located the person's name in your contact list, tap on it to access their details. Ensure that "Allow

Drop-In" is selected under Permissions for a smooth calling experience.

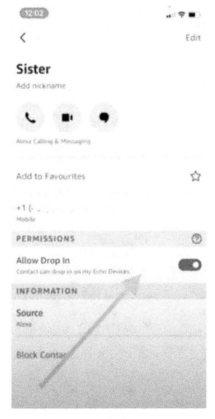

You can easily add individual contacts to your Alexa app, making it convenient to call someone not already in your Amazon address book. It allows greater flexibility and ease of connecting with contacts using your Echo device or the Alexa app.

Video call

Once you've added a person to your contacts, you can easily reach them through video calls, voice calls, or messages. Here's how to access the settings and create a group:

1. To access the settings menu on your Echo Show, swipe down from the top of the screen.
2. From the menu that appears, select "Communication."

3. Next, choose "Show Contacts." If you see "Whose Contacts?" tap your name.
4. Click the "Add New" button to add a contact.

5. Complete the contact information form provided and select the "Save" button to confirm.

6. Please note that even if you add the contact on the Echo Show, you'll still need to ensure that "Drop-in" is turned on in the Alexa app on your phone for seamless communication.

7. The next step is forming a group of the people you've decided upon, making it easier to initiate group calls and stay connected with multiple contacts simultaneously.

Set Up a Group Call

1. Open the Alexa app on your device.

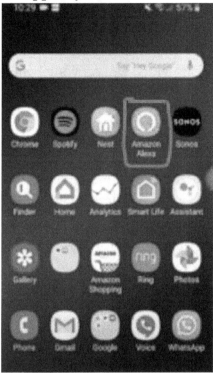

2. Access your contacts list by following the first three steps, as previously mentioned.
3. This time, select "Create New Group."
4. On the next screen, you'll see a list of your contacts. Check the box next to each participant's name to indicate that they should be included in the group call.
5. Once you've selected all the desired participants, tap the "Next" button.

6. Now, you have the opportunity to label the group. Enter a name for the group and then hit the "Create Group" button to finalize the process.

Initiate Group Video Calling

Initiating a group video call on your Echo Show is as simple as saying, "Alexa, call [group name]." Once the call is in progress, the Echo Show's display will provide caller ID and any other relevant information you may need.

However, it's essential to know that what you see on the screen doesn't always reflect your current state during the call. For example, if you see the text "Video On," tapping the corresponding symbol on the screen will activate the video for your caller. But seeing this text doesn't necessarily mean your video has been turned on.

Similarly, you might come across an icon resembling a microphone, indicating that the caller's microphone is muted. You can unmute the caller by tapping this microphone icon.

Understanding these visual cues can help you manage your group video calls more effectively, ensuring that you control your video and audio settings as needed during the conversation.

Enhanced video calling Features

Enhanced Features for video calling on your Echo Show bring fun and creativity to your conversations. You can enjoy using stickers and effects such as a fish tank, googly eyes, flowers, butterflies, and much more, similar to what you find in other chatting apps. These elements add an enjoyable and expressive dimension to your video calls.

However, it's important to note that, for now, group calls are limited to standard capabilities, so you won't be able to use these fun stickers and effects in group conversations. Additionally, live captioning during calls is currently available exclusively for one-on-one conversations, enhancing accessibility and convenience in those interactions.

As technology evolves, more features and capabilities will become available for group calls and other aspects of video calling on Echo devices, offering even more ways to express yourself and connect with others.

Tips for video calls

Now that you know how to engage in video calls, I wish you a wonderful time. To ensure a great experience, it's essential to consider your surroundings. Avoid standing in areas with strong backlighting from windows or lamps, and ensure you're not in complete darkness. Be cautious of direct, intense sunlight on your face, which can lead to overexposure. Everyone involved in the call must have a stable and reasonably fast internet connection to prevent video stuttering.

Fast calling

Initiating a group call with your entire family using Alexa is effortless. Say, "Alexa, call my family group." While setting up a group may take a few minutes initially, it's straightforward.

Once the call is in progress, everyone in the family group will be visible to each other on the screen. It makes it easy to share updates, connect with distant relatives, or even plan a get-together, fostering a sense of togetherness.

When it's time to end the call, you can simply tell Alexa to do so by saying, "Alexa, hang up." Enjoy the convenience of connecting and chatting with your loved ones using your Echo device, making communication within your family group a delightful and hassle-free experience.

Home Monitoring

Using your Echo Show may involve different specifics and available settings, but some fundamental procedures typically apply. Here's how to use the Echo Show, especially for Home Monitoring:

1. To access the settings, swipe down from the upper part of the display, then scroll down and select the "Camera" option.

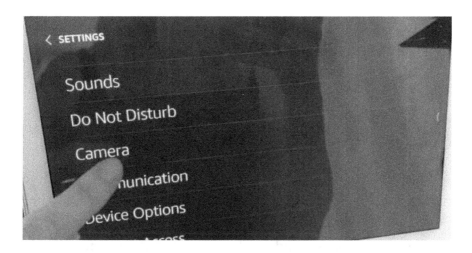

2. To activate Home Monitoring, tap the "On" switch.

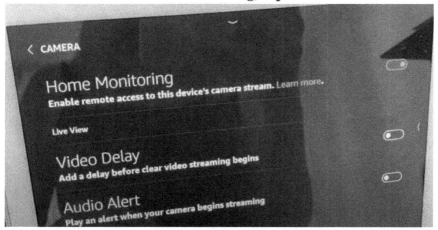

3. Click the continue icon to proceed.
4. You may be asked to enter your Amazon username and password to confirm your identity. A virtual keyboard will appear on the screen for you to enter your password. Sometimes, you might also need to provide a two-factor authentication code for added security.

It's important to note that Home Monitoring on the Echo Show has some limitations. For example, it lacks certain functionalities commonly found in dedicated security cameras, like the ability to record footage. If your goal is to capture specific events or activities, a dedicated video-recording security camera might be more suitable.

The Home Monitoring system also does not send notifications when motion is detected. Some security cameras can send alerts when motion is detected. However, the Echo Show 10 (3rd gen) and later models allow you to set up routines that automatically issue alerts, adding more functionality to your monitoring setup.

Home monitoring Privacy concerns

It's essential to be aware that someone in the same room as an Echo Show, who may not know that Home Monitoring is enabled, could compromise their privacy. To address this concern, Amazon has implemented a feature that displays a notification on the screen whenever Home Monitoring is used. This notification ensures that anyone near the Echo Show can see their camera feed being monitored.

Suppose you are the person who is being monitored or feel that your privacy is being infringed upon. In that case, you can manually turn off the Home Monitoring function by clicking the "Stop" button within the on-screen notification. This way, you can regain your privacy and prevent others from monitoring your activities, even if you believe you're alone in the room.

This feature adds an essential layer of transparency and control, ensuring that individuals are aware of when their camera feed is being accessed and allowing them to take action to protect their privacy if needed.

CHAPTER 5

What are Alexa Routines

The next step to enjoy the full benefits of Alexa routine automation involves setting up your Amazon Echo for multiple users, customizing the wake word, or enabling package tracking. The routines feature on Amazon Echo is both user-friendly and powerful. It involves one or more sequential tasks, allowing you to automate various actions. For example, routines are commonly used for tasks like adjusting lighting and getting news updates.

Without using routines, you'd typically have to give Alexa two separate commands to accomplish these actions: "Alexa, activate the lights" and "Alexa, news briefing." However, you can streamline these tasks with routines into a single command. Plus, you can do more than just these two operations. For instance, you can initiate a routine by saying, "Alexa, work time."

Routines can be tailored to individual needs using specific keywords and a schedule. With the right smart home technology, you can open your blinds automatically while receiving a breaking news briefing. Alternatively, you could use Alexa on your Amazon Echo to activate your coffee maker through a smart socket.

Alexa's intelligent automation capabilities are a significant reason why many people appreciate the platform. Your account can accommodate as many as 99 routines, offering extensive possibilities to simplify and enhance your daily routines.

Customize Alexa Routine

1. Open the Alexa app and access the Routines page by tapping the "More" menu item.
2. To start creating a routine, tap the Plus icon in the upper right corner of the page, or choose "Create Routine" at the bottom.
3. Give your routine a name by selecting "Enter routine name." Once done, click "Next" in the top right corner.
4. Now, you need to specify "When this takes place." Here, you can define the exact trigger for your routine. You can

choose from options like Voice, Schedule, Smart Home Event, Location, or a combination. Select the trigger that suits your habit and click "Next."

5. After choosing the trigger, select "Add action." It is where you define what Alexa will do as part of your routine. You have various options, including Alexa Says, Smart Home, Audible, Fire TV, Music & Podcasts, and more.

6. You can continue adding actions to your routine by selecting the appropriate option and tapping "Next." Custom actions can be added, but they must be placed at the end of the routine.

7. Once you've added all the desired actions, you can save your changes by tapping "Save" in the top right corner.

8. Finally, select the device you want Alexa to respond to. Your routine will start automatically once activated according to the trigger you've set.

You can create personalized habits with Alexa, allowing you to automate various tasks and actions to streamline your daily routines and make them more convenient.

Fantastic Alexa Routines

Creating Alexa routines is a straightforward process, and here are five sample routines to illustrate how easy it is to get started. Let's start with "Get the Day Going":

1. Begin with your morning news briefing, just like you would from a radio alarm clock. Unlike the "Start my day" Featured Routine, which is triggered by a word, this routine can be set to run at a specific time every day, say, 7 a.m. To create this action, select "News."

2. After the news, you can follow up with a weather update and then choose to play music or a podcast.

3. Additionally, you can activate the water heater and a specific light by selecting the "Smart Home" option.

4. Once you've configured these actions, select "Save" to activate the routine.

With these simple steps, you can set up an Alexa routine to kickstart your day with a morning news briefing, weather update, and your choice of music or podcast. Plus, you can control other smart home devices to enhance your morning routine further. Alexa routines offer convenience and customization to suit your daily needs.

Wishing You a Happy Birthday

While it requires proactive planning, you can surprise yourself or a dear one with a heartfelt birthday message from Alexa. Here's a step-by-step guide on how to set this up:

1. Begin by organizing your week in advance, ensuring your daily tasks are well-managed.

2. When the special day arrives, summon Alexa to deliver the birthday wishes. To do this, navigate to Alexa's actions and select "Phrases."

3. Within the "Phrases" menu, specifically look for the "Birthday" category. Here, you can choose from a simple "Happy Birthday" greeting or opt for more elaborate and personalized messages.

4. For an even more heartfelt touch, select "Alexa says," then go the extra mile by choosing "Custom" and crafting your birthday message in your own words. This

personalization adds a unique and thoughtful element to the birthday surprise.

You can create a memorable and special birthday moment using Alexa's capabilities. It's a thoughtful way to celebrate and make someone's day even more extraordinary.

Change mood

Alexa boasts compatibility with various smart lighting systems, although navigating its operations solely through voice commands can pose some challenges. For instance, when you request Alexa to illuminate the room, you might encounter a somewhat sassy AI retort, with an artificial voice quipping, "I've spotted multiple lights; which one are you referring to?" all the while, the room remains in darkness.

However, fret not, for there exists a relatively straightforward method to configure Alexa for efficient lighting management sans the need for intricate specifications. Kickstart your day with a simple mention, such as "working during the day" or "relaxing in the evening."

Surprisingly, while the customary wake word remains imperative for issuing commands, it curiously becomes optional in this context. Opt for "Smart Home" as the trigger, and then fine-tune the ambiance by adjusting parameters like intensity, hue, and color temperature. Once satisfied with your settings, don't hesitate to assign a multitude of functions to each lamp according to your preferences.

This innovative lighting routine feature empowers you to orchestrate simultaneous adjustments across numerous lights and other smart devices. The possibility even extends to delegating commands to multiple scenes or groups, making your smart lighting experience more versatile and user-friendly.

Welcome Home

Indeed, it's a great idea to include a friendly "good evening" as part of your routine when you arrive home from work, creating a warm and welcoming atmosphere. Here's how you can set this up with Alexa:

1. Start by selecting "Alexa says" and then "Phrases."
2. Choose a suitable phrase or term, such as "I'm home," from the provided options. You can even request Alexa to select a sentence at random to keep it interesting.
3. If you have smart home devices like a motion detector at your doorway, you can incorporate them into your routine. Set up a trigger that activates when you enter your home so Alexa greets you automatically.
4. Alternatively, you can establish a location-based routine if you have the Alexa app on your phone. Select "Location" from the "When this happens" drop-down menu and pick a departure or arrival event. Provide your home address to trigger the routine when you enter your house.

Remember that for location-based routines via the Alexa app, you'll need to grant the app permission to access your location.

You can make your arrival home a pleasant and personalized experience with Alexa extending a warm greeting as you walk through the door.

Traffic Report

Before we wrap up our day, let's establish a fresh habit using Alexa, involving timers or voice activation. Imagine this scenario: You're all set to hit the road, and you want to stay informed about traffic conditions. Here's how to set up this helpful routine:

1. Start by asking Alexa, "Alexa, what's my traffic?"
2. Next, select the "Traffic" option and add it as an action.
3. Remember to save your newly created routine.

While this may seem routine on the surface, there's more to it than meets the eye. You'll need to tweak your daily schedule to incorporate this feature into your life seamlessly. Doing so informs Alexa about your commute starting and ending points and lets her know if you plan to make any pit stops along the way.

To fine-tune Alexa's settings for this traffic feature, follow these steps:

1. Open the menu drawer and click on "More."

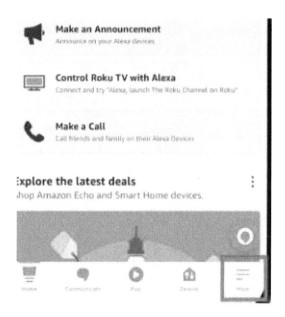

2. Find the "Traffic" button and click it.

3. Fill out the "to" and "from" columns in the ensuing interface with your specific commute details.

With this, it's possible to harness Alexa's capabilities to streamline your daily commute and avoid any potential traffic snarls. It's about making your routine more efficient and stress-free.

Share routines

Sharing routines with others through the Alexa app is a convenient way to enhance their smart home experience or streamline their daily tasks. Here's how you can share a routine:

1. Open the Alexa app and go to the "Routines" menu.

2. To send a routine to someone else, open the specific routine you want to share.
3. In the upper right corner of the routine screen, click on the three dots (ellipsis icon).
4. From the options that appear, select "Share Routine."
5. You can now disseminate the routine to others through various methods, including phone, email, or the web.

You can easily share your customized routines with friends, family members, or anyone who can benefit from the automation and convenience of Alexa routines.

Create Voice ID

To set up your Voice ID for Alexa, follow these steps carefully:

1. Open the Alexa application on your mobile device.

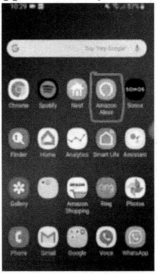

2. Ensure that the correct person is signed in to the Alexa app because the Voice ID you create will be linked to the account currently logged in.
3. To check if you're signed in correctly, tap the "More" button in the bottom menu bar of the app.

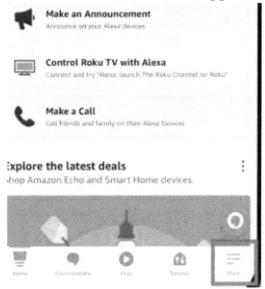

4. From there, navigate to "Settings" and then "Your Profile & Family." Make sure the heading under your name reads "Your Profile."

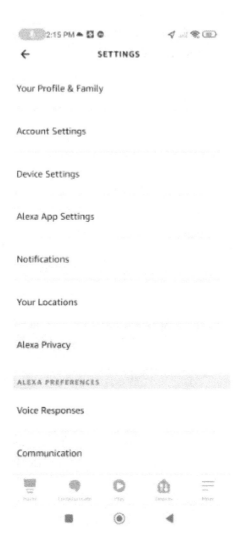

5. Once you've confirmed the correct profile, tap your name, and you will find the "Voice ID setup" option.
6. You won't have access to this menu after completing your Voice ID setup.
7. The screen will indicate your profile is ready if your voice is successfully detected during the setup. If you need to

start over, select "Voice ID" from the menu, then choose "Delete Voice ID" on the next screen, and finally, select the "Voice ID setup" option again.

8. Press the "Agree" and "Continue" icons on the Voice ID setup screen to proceed with the setup.

Teach Alexa your voice.

1. Start with the initial phrase displayed on the screen and say it to Alexa. Alexa will then provide the next phrase.
2. Continue this process, repeating each phrase as instructed by Alexa until you've completed all the options provided.
3. If Alexa doesn't accurately capture a phrase on the first try, don't worry; she will ask you to repeat it.
4. Once you've completed this setup process, Alexa will confirm creating your Voice ID.
5. To finish, choose the "Done" option.

Verify Name Pronunciation

Once you've set up your Voice ID, the next step is to ensure that Alexa correctly pronounces your first name. Here's how you can do it:

1. To change how your name is displayed on your profile, navigate to the "Edit Name and Pronunciation" page within the Alexa app.
2. On the subsequent screen, look for the button labeled "Go to Saved Pronunciation" at the bottom.
3. To hear Alexa say your name, press the "Play" button next to it.

4. If Alexa's pronunciation isn't quite correct, click the "Let's Fix That" button. You can experiment with various pronunciations of your name to find the one that sounds the best.

5. Alternatively, you can choose the "Write it out" option and manually enter the correct pronunciation. When Alexa responds correctly, you can tap "That's Better." If Alexa nails it on the first try, you can select "Nailed it."

CHAPTER 6

Connect Music Streaming Platforms

T he Alexa app requires you to link your chosen music streaming service before you can enjoy music through it. Accessing Amazon Music and potentially other services is done by navigating to "More" > "Settings" > "Music & Podcasts" within the app. From there, select the service you want to add to your Echo device and press "Link New Service." Once you're all set up, you can instruct Alexa to play your preferred tunes or use your preferred music streaming app with your Echo as the playback destination. Some popular music apps can seamlessly work together with Alexa in this manner.

Add Spotify

To fully unlock the potential of Spotify on your Echo device, it's crucial to have a Spotify Premium subscription, which typically costs $9.99 per month. Users with the free Spotify tier can access only limited features, such as specific playlists like "Today's Top Hits" or "Discover Weekly."

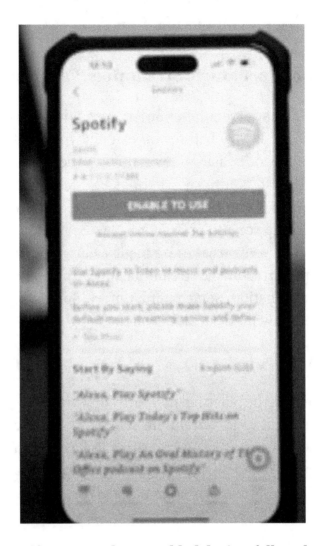

To add Spotify to your Alexa-enabled device, follow these steps: Go to the "Link New Services" page in the Alexa app, select Spotify, press "Enable to Use," and log in to your Spotify account. During this setup, Alexa may request permission to access your Spotify information. Granting this permission ensures a seamless integration, enabling Alexa to effortlessly control your Spotify account and provide a seamless music streaming experience.

Add Pandora

Adding Pandora to your Echo device is a breeze. Begin by selecting Pandora from the available services in the "Link New Service" menu within the Alexa app. Once you've chosen Pandora, activate it by pressing the "Enable to Use" button on the Pandora Skills page.

To grant Alexa access to your Pandora account, enter your login details. After setting up your account on your Echo device, you'll receive confirmation on the Pandora Alexa Skill page that the two services are now seamlessly connected. To dive into your favorite tunes, press the "Done" button, and you're all set to enjoy Pandora's musical wonders through your Echo device.

Include Deezer

To integrate Deezer with Alexa, follow these steps: Begin by pressing the Deezer symbol to access your account. To extend this feature to your smartphone:

1. Navigate to the skills page and select the "Enable to activate" option.
2. Allow Alexa access to your Deezer account by logging in and pressing the "Accept" icon.
3. Once you've completed these steps, select "Done" to commence your musical journey.

After adding your preferred music services, navigate to the Alexa app's Music page and scroll down to find your newly added services prominently displayed. Instructing Alexa to play music from various services is a breeze with this setup. For instance, you can say, "Alexa, play Moon Walk from Apple Music" or "Alexa, play the news from iHeartRadio," and Alexa will promptly oblige. To avoid mix-ups, designate a preferred service that Alexa will consistently use by incorporating its name into the default configuration. You can easily customize Alexa's behavior by tapping "Default Services." Furthermore, you can instruct Alexa to play music by a specific artist, such as the Beatles or Beethoven, or by genre, like rock or jazz, by adjusting the default settings for artist and genre. This level of customization allows you to effortlessly command Alexa to play a specific track, album, artist, genre, or radio station, and she will seamlessly fulfill your request.

Create IFTTT Account

It all begins with creating an account on the IFTTT website. If you can't find Alexa prominently displayed, a simple search will lead you to it, followed by clicking the "Connect" button. To link your Amazon and IFTTT accounts, follow the provided instructions. You might need to sign in to additional services like Apple or Google, depending on your needs.

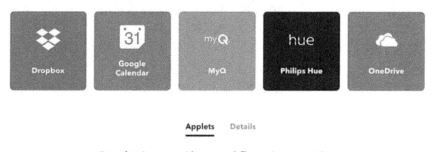

It's worth noting that the free IFTTT account allows for up to five applets at a time, but if you require more, you can opt for IFTTT Pro, which offers twenty applets and is available for $3 per month or $24 per year. Once everything is set up, you can install pre-made applets that suit your preferences by selecting

"Create." This user-friendly approach empowers you to enhance your Alexa experience, tailor interactions, and automate tasks to align with your unique requirements and smart home ecosystem.

Use IFTTT

An IFTTT applet to operate seamlessly requires both "If This" and "Then That" components. In this context, "If This" can be tailored to match your specific Alexa command.

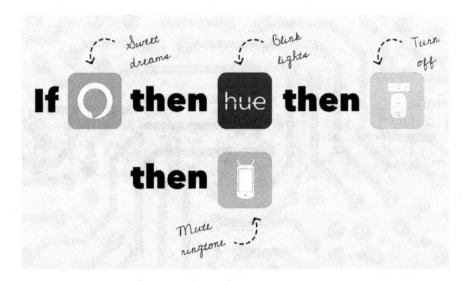

To set up this interaction, start by selecting "Amazon Alexa" from the menu that appears after clicking the "Add" button next to "If This." Then, explore the range of available triggers. While there are over a dozen ways to activate Alexa, the core concept is relatively straightforward:

Essentially, "say a specific phrase" translates to creating a customized voice command that can be triggered by uttering

"Alexa, trigger (voice command)." It lets you initiate a personalized action based on your unique needs and preferences.

Alexa's capabilities extend beyond direct voice commands; it can also activate more intricate IFTTT triggers. For instance, it can be set to respond when you create a new shopping list or to-do item, start playing a new song, or request information about a sports score. These are just a few examples of the diverse ways Alexa can serve as a catalyst for IFTTT applets, providing users a versatile and tailored experience.

Select IFTTT Outcomes

It is where IFTTT excels, enabling you to perform tasks surpassing Alexa's capabilities.

Select the device, platform, or service you want to connect to your Alexa routines to unleash this power. Press the "Add" button next to "Then That." The beauty of IFTTT lies in its compatibility with an extensive array of other services, opening doors to diverse possibilities. You can seamlessly integrate email and messaging apps such as Discord and Slack, collaborate with file-sharing platforms like Box, Dropbox, and Google Drive, manage tasks using to-do list managers like Evernote and OneNote, or even control your smart home systems like Nest and Google Home. It's versatile enough to handle standard SMS messaging as well. Remember that for any automation you wish to establish, you'll require an active IFTTT account, and you must link all the services and platforms you intend to utilize to that account.

Once you've chosen the specific service or device you want IFTTT to communicate with, the next step involves specifying the exact nature of this interaction. As you proceed to the next page after selecting a platform, you'll encounter a range of options tailored to that platform. It is where the intricacies come into play.

While controlling smart home devices involves straightforward actions like locking or unlocking a door or toggling lights on or off, more complex scenarios require finesse. To achieve your desired results, you must meticulously fill in the relevant fields and incorporate any necessary IFTTT Ingredients, ensuring that the automation aligns perfectly with your requirements and expectations. It's within these details that the true potential and versatility of IFTTT indeed come to life.

Save IFTTT

The final steps are straightforward. Just click "Continue" to progress with the setup. Here, you can choose whether to receive push alerts via the IFTTT app whenever the applet activates, providing you with real-time notifications. Once you've made this decision, click "Finish," your applet is primed and ready for action. With this seamless integration, Alexa can execute your customized applet, responding to your voice commands and triggering the designated actions.

The world of applets within IFTTT offers boundless possibilities and creative experimentation. For those who relish diving into innovative automation, an IFTTT Pro account becomes a compelling option. It unlocks advanced features like fine-tuning events with queries and filters, providing a higher level of customization. However, if your needs primarily revolve around everyday tasks and routines, a primary account with limited options often proves sufficient. The choice between these account types ultimately depends on your appetite for exploration and the complexity of the automation you intend to create. It's a journey of customization and convenience adaptable to both the curious and the pragmatist.

Modify Background

To customize the wallpaper on your Echo Show, you can access the Alexa app on your mobile device. Open the app, tap "More" in the bottom right corner, then go to "Settings" > "Device Settings." From there, select your Echo Show device, and under its settings, find the "Picture Show" option. You can link your Echo Show to photo libraries from Facebook, Amazon Photos, or your mobile device.

You have various customization choices, including selecting a single image as wallpaper, enabling "Daily Memories" or "This Day" to see highlights, and connecting associated services like Facebook or Amazon Photos. Alternatively, you can make these adjustments directly on the Echo Show by using voice commands or accessing the settings menu. This flexibility lets you personalize your Echo Show's display with your favorite photos and memories.

Configure Silks settings

You'll find that Silk, Amazon's web browser, comes preloaded when using most Amazon Fire tablets and smartphones. However, before browsing the web, it's crucial to ensure that Silk is configured to execute your commands effectively. To do this, follow these steps:

1. Start by opening the Settings menu on your device.
2. Within the Settings menu, locate and select "Web Options."
3. Next, click "Browser," then proceed to "Browser Settings."

Silk offers a variety of features and settings that can enhance your browsing experience. These include page scaling, which ensures web pages are displayed correctly on your screen, password storage for convenience, protection against potentially malicious websites to keep you safe, and the ability to delete your browsing history and cookies for privacy.

Furthermore, you can customize your search engine to suit your preferences better. Under the "Advanced Settings" tab, you can swap out the default search engine, Bing, for alternatives like Google, Yahoo, or DuckDuckGo. This small but significant adjustment can substantially impact your browsing experience, allowing you to use the search engine you're most comfortable with.

By taking a few moments to configure Silk's settings, you can ensure that your web browsing on Amazon devices, including the Echo Show, is seamless and tailored to your preferences. This level of customization empowers you to make the most out of your browsing experience while enjoying the features and capabilities that Silk offers.

Adjust sounds Levels

The Echo Show offers an equalizer feature that allows you to adjust the balance of low, mid, and high frequencies to enhance your audio experience. You can access this equalizer through the device's settings menu by selecting "Sounds" and then the "Equalizer" option.

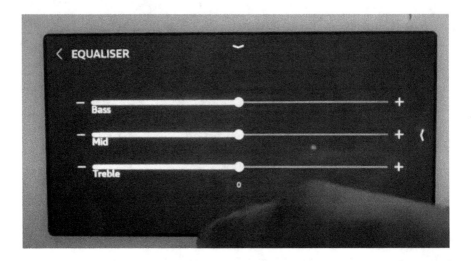

Alternatively, you can use the mobile Alexa app to adjust the equalizer settings for your specific Echo Show device.

The equalizer sliders can be manually adjusted to your desired positions, or you can use voice commands like "Alexa, adjust the treble" or "Alexa, lower the bass" to make real-time audio adjustments. If you ever want to revert to the default settings, a voice command such as "Alexa, reset the equalizer" will do the trick. This feature ensures you control your audio preferences and can tailor the sound output to your liking, whether you're using an Echo Show with a screen or another Echo device.

Karaoke

If you're an Amazon Prime member, the Echo Show opens the door to a musical world with access to over 2 million songs from Amazon's extensive music library, and this is included as part of your Prime membership. However, you're looking to broaden your musical horizons further and delve into a library of over 75 million tracks.

In that case, Amazon offers an additional subscription service called Amazon Music Unlimited for a nominal fee. What makes the Echo Show's music experience even more engaging is its ability to display real-time lyrics for a substantial portion of these songs, presenting them line by line as the music plays. It adds a new dimension to your music enjoyment, allowing you to sing along or immerse yourself in the lyrics.

Moreover, the Echo Show provides convenient touch controls that put you in the driver's seat of your musical journey. You can effortlessly play, pause, or skip tracks within an album or playlist. Feeling spontaneous? Create a shuffled playlist for some musical surprises. And if you have a particular playlist that's just perfect, you can set it to repeat.

It's worth noting that while Amazon Music offers this impressive lyrics feature, some rival music streaming services like Pandora and Spotify, unfortunately, do not provide lyrics display on the Echo Show. So, if you're a music enthusiast and love to explore songs more interactively, Amazon Music on your Echo Show is a compelling choice.

Set screen brightness

To enable the Echo's Do Not Disturb mode or instruct Alexa by saying, "Alexa, do not disturb," you can conveniently swipe down from the top of the screen. Once activated, the Do Not

Disturb mode dims the lights temporarily, ensuring that your movements won't activate any unwanted illumination.

An exciting feature is the screen's brightness adjustment, which can be fine-tuned using a slider ranging from one to ten. This slider lets you set the screen's brightness to your preferred level, with the maximum setting achievable through this method. For instance, if you say, "Alexa, set brightness to 10," Alexa will provide guidance, prompting you to scroll down the screen to adjust. This user-friendly approach allows you to customize your Echo Show's display settings effortlessly.

Watch YouTube

When you first inquire about launching a web browser on Alexa, you'll be prompted to choose a default browser. Amazon Silk and Mozilla Firefox are among the options available. You can skip this step for future YouTube requests by tapping your preferred browser.

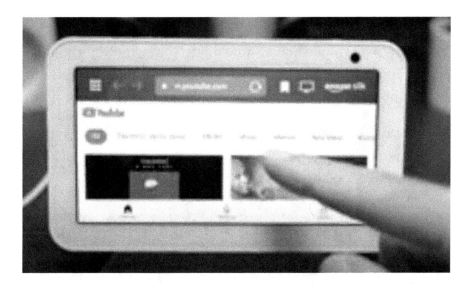

It's worth noting that Firefox, like Chrome, is one of the few browsers that supports YouTube TV. Therefore, you can still access YouTube TV content if you prefer Firefox over Silk.

Alexa will initiate your selected web browser and load YouTube upon your request. Whether to use your YouTube account or not is entirely up to you. Once set up, you can easily instruct Alexa to open YouTube on your Echo Show, and the website will load seamlessly. Navigating YouTube is as intuitive as using a tablet's touchscreen; you can sign in and browse YouTube content effortlessly using the Echo Show's touchscreen.

For instance, when you request, "Alexa, play SNL on YouTube," Alexa will perform a search and present you with a results page directly from YouTube. From there, you can select the video you wish to watch, making the process of enjoying YouTube content on your Echo Show a breeze.

Update software

In some cases, older Echo Show models may require the latest software update to access certain features, such as YouTube. Here's how you can check for and apply software updates:

1. Swipe down from the top of the Echo Show's screen to access the menu.
2. Select "Settings" from the menu options.

3. Within the Settings menu, navigate to the "Device Options" section.
4. Look for the "Software Updates" option and select it.
5. If there are any available software updates, you'll have the option to apply them. Be sure to install any necessary upgrades.
6. After applying the updates, the Echo Show will refresh, and you should now be able to access YouTube and other features that require the latest software version.

Configure Netflix App

Enjoying your favorite series and movies on your Amazon Echo Show is a breeze, thanks to the ability to sign in to your Netflix account. Here's how you can get started with just a few clicks:

1. Ensure your Echo Show is powered on and ready.
2. Swipe left from the right edge of the screen. This action will reveal a menu with quick-access options. However, please note that on older Echo Show models, you may need to swipe down from the upper part of the display to access these shortcuts.
3. Once the menu appears, select "Video" from the available options.

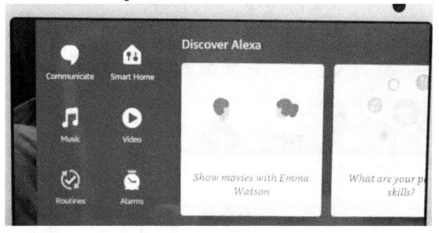

4. If you intend to watch content on Netflix, you'll find it listed among the available streaming providers. In most cases, there's no need to download Netflix separately since it usually comes pre-installed on Amazon Echo Show devices.

5. After selecting Netflix, you'll be prompted to log in with your Netflix account credentials.

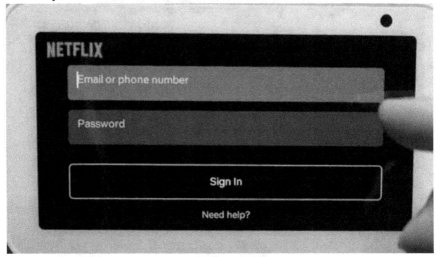

6. Once you've done that, you'll be all set to start watching your desired videos without any delay.

With these straightforward steps, you can easily access and enjoy your Netflix content on your Amazon Echo Show, making it a convenient and enjoyable experience.

Watch Netflix

Connect your Echo Show to Wi-Fi, then say, "Alexa, open Netflix." When you launch Netflix, you'll be prompted to sign in before you can start watching videos.

After logging into Netflix on the Echo Show, voice commands you can use to browse for movies, play, stop, and rewind them. The loudness can be adjusted by simply raising or lowering your voice. Say it;

- Say, "Alexa, stream The Harder They Fall"
- Say, "Alexa, pause." Use the phrase "Alexa, rewind 10 seconds.' Saying, "Alexa, lower the volume."

Connect Wi-Fi to Alexa

To set up your Alexa device and connect it to Wi-Fi using the Alexa app or a web browser, follow these steps:

Using the Alexa App:

1. Open the Alexa app and ensure that your Alexa device is in pairing or setup mode (usually indicated by a blinking light).
2. Go to the "Devices" menu, indicated by a plus sign (+).
3. Choose "Add Device" and select the type of device you're setting up. If your Alexa device is discoverable, it may appear automatically, and you can follow the on-screen instructions.
4. If you need to add your device manually, select it from the list provided.
5. Follow the on-screen instructions, which may include selecting your Wi-Fi network and entering the password when prompted.
6. Your Alexa device will connect to Wi-Fi and the internet through the app.

Using a Web Browser:

1. Ensure that your Alexa device is in pairing or setup mode (usually indicated by a blinking light).
2. Open a web browser on a desktop or laptop computer (Firefox, Edge, or Safari, as Chrome is incompatible).
3. Visit the website alexa.amazon.com and log in with your Amazon credentials.
4. In the left-hand menu, select "Settings."
5. Click on "Install new hardware."

6. Choose your specific Alexa device with a unique Wi-Fi identifier (e.g., Amazon-XXX).
7. Follow the on-screen instructions, including selecting your private Wi-Fi network and entering your Wi-Fi credentials.
8. Your Alexa device will automatically connect to Wi-Fi and the internet.

Following these steps, you can successfully set up your Alexa device and ensure it's connected to your Wi-Fi network and the internet. You can refer to Alexa troubleshooting instructions for assistance if you encounter connectivity issues.

Modify Wi-Fi settings

1. Start the Alexa app on your smartphone or tablet.
2. Ensure your phone is connected to the same Wi-Fi network you want your Alexa device to connect to.
3. On the app's main screen, select "Devices" from the menu at the bottom.
4. At the top of the screen, tap "Echo & Alexa."
5. From the drop-down menu, choose your specific Alexa device.
6. To adjust device settings, tap the gear icon within the device panel.
7. In the "Wi-Fi Network" section, select "Change" to enter the setup or pairing mode. The exact steps may vary depending on your specific Alexa device.
8. Follow the on-screen instructions, which may include selecting your new Wi-Fi network from the list of available networks and entering its credentials.

CONCLUSION

It's evident that the Echo Show 5 is not just a device; it's a lifestyle upgrade. With the knowledge and skills you've gained, you're well on your way to mastering this remarkable device, unlocking its full potential, and seamlessly integrating it into your daily life. With each update, it evolves, offering new features and enhancements.

Your journey with the Echo Show 5 has only just begun. The possibilities are boundless, and as you explore, experiment, and personalize your experience, you'll find that this device is a constant companion, simplifying your life, enhancing your entertainment, and connecting you to the world in remarkable ways.

www.ingramcontent.com/pod-product-compliance
Lightning Source LLC
LaVergne TN
LVHW051711050326
832903LV00032B/4129

ISBN 9798866583270

90000

9 798866 583270